WHERE I LIVE

Poems by
Pat Underwood

BLUE LIGHT PRESS ◆ 1ST WORLD PUBLISHING

1st WORLD
PUBLISHING

SAN FRANCISCO ◆ FAIRFIELD ◆ DELHI

Finalist, 2022 Blue Light Book Award

Where I Live

Copyright ©2022, Pat Underwood

BLUE LIGHT PRESS
www.bluelightpress.com
bluelightpress@aol.com

1ST WORLD PUBLISHING
PO Box 2211
Fairfield, IA 52556
www.1stworldpublishing.com

BOOK & COVER DESIGN
Melanie Gendron
melaniegendron999@gmail.com

COVER ART
Cloud Play by Gary Bowling

AUTHOR PHOTO
Penny Zaugg

FIRST EDITION

Library of Congress Cataloging-in-Publication Data

ISBN: 978-1-4218-3524-2

WHERE I LIVE

Acknowledgments

With deep appreciation, I wish to thank the editors of the following magazines and anthologies in which my poems first appeared, some with altered titles:

The Briar Cliff Review: "Burn Pile," "Metaphor for My Grandfather," "The Dinner Party," "Vicksburg"

Dog Haiku Chapbook: "pinprick of moonlight"

Encore Prize Poems: "Colostomy," "For a Short While, We Actually Liked Geometry," "Wooden Slats and Lavender"

Expressions Literary Magazine: "Calling Paul"

Lyrical Iowa: "After Surgery DT's," "Bypass," "Hooves," "In this Ethiopian restaurant," "Resilience," "Sea Senses; Cancun, Mexico"

Midwest Federation of Chaparral Poets; Iowa Chapter: "Barn Swallows," "Epithalamium"

Midwest Poetry Review: "Angels in the Corn"

National League of American Pen Women: "Argument for Wetlands," "Night Noises"

Opus Literary Review: "Where I Live"

Poetic Page: "Ice Caves," "Under My Care"

River King: "Along Elliot Bay," "Barn Swallows," "Biology Field Trip; Ankeny, IA"

Stand Alone: "Trinity"

Voices from the Prairie/Iowa Public Radio: "Where I Live"

Voices International: "At Water's Edge"

Author's Note

Many thanks to Blue Light Press, editor Diane Frank, book designer Melanie Gendron, and the entire book team for the publication of this book. Thank you to Gary Bowling for his generous gift of the cover art *Cloud Play* and also to Francine Witte for her contribution toward this publication. I'm indebted to my friends in various writing groups whose support means the world to me. I especially want to thank Jeanne Emmons, Phil Hey, and Bill Rudolph for their nurturance and insight. Loretta Walker inspired its creation. Finally, it was a joy working with Michael Carey and his wise critique of this manuscript.

To Michael Carey,
teacher and friend

Keep some room in your heart
for the unimaginable.
– Mary Oliver 1935 – 2019

Contents

WOODEN SLATS AND LAVENDER

ICE CAVES

Barefoot in the summer,

we were fearless.
Hay stubble in the fields,
slimy mud from the rains,
climbing every rugged tree.

The orchard was behind us –
pear, cherry, peach,
a leaf turned golden,
a wren calling to another.

When the apples ripened
and we bit through the tender skin,
we pretended our tomorrows
would be bright as the sunshine
landing on our bare toes.

Life had a way of clouding up,
but you remained my cheerful
antagonist, my protector.
Even at your deathbed
you knew I'd be there,
smiling among the tears,

barefoot in summer again
laughing at your silly antics
and nothing, nothing
ever being able to take that away.

Metamorphosis

Furry caterpillar tickling my palm,
climbing my arm
in this June sunshine.
It's mysterious how she molts,
how she has fake legs and real legs,
how she has fake eyes and real eyes.

I place her in the grass.
She crawls away, sheds her skin,
catches the silk button above her head,
suspends in air. Ready now,
she forms a chrysalis.

When the waiting air coaxes her
to throw away her husk,
her wings, soft, damp, folded,
fill with blood. She's a leaf
lifting from an oak branch,

sweeping from stamen to stamen,
pistil to pistil. I watch
her black and gold flutter
above wood ducks and mallards
at the river spill,
tremble dandelion's bright yellow.

Like my mother when she forgave
our childish ways,
slipping into beautiful wings.

Testing for Moisture

My father stepped into the field that spring
and sifted black earth through his fingers
until it fell to the ground like a kiss
to that which fed us, clothed us,
put a roof over our heads.

Toby stood in the nearby grass,
tail wagging, eyes watching –
ever the approving companion
for an Iowa farmer and his yields,
so fertile, with only our silence,
as usual, and Mother's steaming stew,
cornbread and butter on the side.

Even now I think of my father
loving, cursing each ambivalent bump
his tractor would feel –
the miracle of growth on the farm
that fed a hungry world.

Ice Caves

And I recall his hands, two measures
of tenderness he laid against my face…
                – Li-Young Lee

We searched everywhere in the tall snow
until we found a bank high enough
for the three of us to fit.
The mound was solid and wet,
and when we dug a hole in the side
and walked into the hollow,
the walls held firm.
Perhaps it was Grandfather's teaching
that spurred my father on.
Whatever it was, he tilted his head low
in his fur-lined cap, and our eyes widened
as he shaped a block of ice into a seat.
We watched his hands, like an artist's.
How's that? he asked. *It's perfect!*
And the raw wind whipped
and whistled and whined
outside the igloo warmth of our cave.

In New Orleans

The Mississippi's silver flutter
trails under a bridge.
Clouds flit above feathery trees.

I am a child again,
walking down our country creek,
toes slithery in mud.
A dragonfly is blue
against summer's light,
a grasshopper's legs
the green, green leaves.

Floating in innocence
I understand love:
creek banks printed with paws,
chirps of robins full-throated in air.

I am wading under the bridge
to the concrete slab.
My brothers join me,
our bare feet numbed
in the water's icy flow.

Calling Paul

in memory of my father

A southern cousin,
you weren't used to hills
with snow stacked in layers
like wool blankets,
but you drove our roads
to shake Father's hand,
to taste the richness
of Mother's beef stew.

You slid into our ditch,
landing soft as an infant
placed in his cradle,
blushing when Father
pulled out your car.

Over the register's iron grate,
you rubbed chilled palms,
the unsteady puffs
warm and welcome.

It seemed a short stay,
time melting like spring thaw
as we talked late into night,
as we played Crazy 8.

This morning,
I call to tell you the news.
It's 80 degrees,
but I feel a snowstorm in my bones.
Slowly, we will wait
for this coldness to clear,
this June of my father's passing.

Making Noodles

in memory of Grandmother

Flour, salt, eggs, butter,
a few tablespoons of cream in a bowl.

Grandmother was always organized:
towels in place on their rack,

apron tied neat at her back.
We mixed the ingredients together,

dusted flour on cheesecloth.
Grandmother's voice

was soft as the dough we kneaded,
fingers patient

as she taught me to slice and turn,
to dry the ribbons into dinner

with mashed potatoes, chicken,
corn on the cob,

and strawberry shortcake for later.
Taste was the sweet arrival

of Grandmother's plan for me –
a life forever tender.

Bending Over the Daffodils

in memory of Grammy

It's as if you were always bending over
the lemon daffodils,
giving the trumpet faces a drink of water,
bringing us horseradish
dug from nearby ditches.

In springtime, I knelt with you.
We dug white-rooted dandelion greens,
watched earth fall from our trowels
like clumps of sweet, brown sugar.

In summer, we peeled and sliced fruit
to make apple butter.

Only you could boil the toughness
from an old hen,
and you brought us pigeon stew,
hot and creamy.

I thought you'd killed the pigeon,
climbing up the hayloft,
shooing one down from the cupola
like a lithe hunter.

You, my dear Grammy,
always found the thirsty face.

Metaphor for My Grandfather

...Amazed, while a small worm lisped to me
The song of my marrow-bones.
— Stanley Kunitz

At the corner of the east field
an earthworm labors in the sod.
Its eyespots, thread of air,
sew into the thickened soil –
so light the sense of touch
that lifts the heavy burden.

Their instincts are to burrow,
to resurrect the holy ground,
at last splashing
into the open door of light,
sunshine swirling
in the golden bath of summer.

Vicksburg

in memory of Fred Armbruster,
my great-grandfather

You listen to soft harmonica strains
of *John Brown's Body* as you sit

hot, bored in the Yankee trench,
waiting out the siege.

Down to only mule meat and peas,
blacks, whites pack together

in earthen cellars
like quaking gazelles in cages.

Outside, magnolias bloom in shades
of whites, pinks, and purple.

Hearing the mockingbird's weaving mimic
among quieted rifle fire and cannon,

you pray this darkness will be forgiven
in Mississippi thickets.

As terms are discussed you leave the ditch,
give coffee and salt to the enemy.

The next day, Vicksburg surrenders.
You clean mildew from your tent,

move from the muddy bayous,
leave the Delta grey-eyed and singing.

For a Short While,
We Actually Liked Geometry

…Laughter our first noun…
— Maxine Kumin

He stood at the chalkboard
and with a short piece of white chalk,
drew angle CED congruent to angle XYZ.
Moving along, suppose we wish to prove
that the sum of the measures…

Mr. Reinfeld droned on. Our eyes glazed over.
I remember Ed Watson's face when he told us,
Down at Lover's Lane! With Miss Thompson!

We imagined Mr. Reinfeld naked from then on.
The shape, size, and position
of geometric figures took on new meaning.

True to the nature of practical applications
and school boards in those days,
Mr. Reinfeld and Miss Thompson were fired.

Later, we did our best
to study hypotenuse and axioms,
but geometry was never the same after that —
just a collection of summations, equations,
and no more explosions.

WHERE I LIVE

Where I Live

Surrounded by woods,
        one flake of snow offers no stability.

Like viewing an artist's canvas,
        enough brush marks force the onlooker

to see the fur of hoarfrost
        as it clings windward to oak's snowy stem.

I am small as I travel these white-painted hills.
        I know the secret caves of molting owls,

the great mine openings deer avoid,
        where nuthatch turn bellies skyward in simple ease.

Even in the cold, jays breasted in soot
        are warm enough here,

fluttering like leaves in trees
        before they hear the pierced chill of hunter's shots

to soar north in strokes blue as arrows –
        souls floating in a sunlit tide of air.

The Shape of Living

...and the soft hues that stain the wild bird's wing,
and flush the clouds when the sun sets.
                          – Henry Wadsworth Longfellow

Out my window
glaciers have sculpted this hill
with neighboring ponds.
Today, the rains have jeweled them.
A pair of wood ducks
glide to my oak tree from the storm,
rest on the branches.

I watch four wild turkeys
run for shelter in the back meadow.
Deer join them, white tails bobbing.
Oh, the song of the wind
as she sings her many languages –
how softly she brushes the cedars.

Beavers keep house at the river –
the nervous gnaw to patch the lodge
with mud and sticks
to seal it tight for winter, to live there
and raise their babies
with the sound of rushing water
soothing their ears.

I grill salmon and bake lemon pie.
When quiet settles over sunset
evening turns to velvet.
I lie down to the chatter of racoons
talking across the timbers.
The rhythm of sleep joins me
like an old friend playing checkers.

Pulling Thistle

This hill is the earth of generations,
the flint of Sac and Fox,
Chief Poweshiek, deer scent
reverent across his back.

A story of gold bullion
lives among stove-lid remnants
where a town breathed,
where men stroked the violin
and stagecoach wheels rutted a trail
through white multi-floral rose.

Before the pasture and its easy graze,
before I borrowed this land
for a moment in time –
dry grass crinkling under my toes,
lavender heads nodding,
waving at the fence line,
the toss of thistle into the burning barrel,

glaciers moved, melted, shaped
these hills into paradise.

Angels in the Corn

Here in the middle
of cornfields stretched
like a green ocean
two men in Levis
come from nowhere
to change my flat.
I watch their hands
elevate the jack,
grip the tire iron,
slacken the wheel.

A shimmer of blonde sunlight
reaches the farm caps
resting on their heads
like faint halos.

Country Road

It could be the scents of summer:
this clover,
these hay fields mowed clean.
It could be the way the sun
touches the horizon
in its mosaic of blues and reds.

Whatever it is, I am audience.

From the nakedness of winter
this society dresses itself green.
Deep thickets of elderberry
line ditches.

Snake grass, wild and outstretched,
slithers along the creek bank.
Tonight, I hear a doe breathing,
the shuffle of hooves in nearby grass.

A killdeer runs ahead, drops her wings –
a ploy for me to follow,
to leave her nest alone.

I think of my sons forging new paths.
Even the killdeer slips off to a cornfield,
goes a new direction.

Soon the moon will be luminous
as night arrives
and wind brushes my cheek.

Hooves

Tonight, dusk wraps my shoulders
like a warm shawl. I am mowing the ditch
and slip a little at steepness.

I hear hooves dig the yard above me,
and suddenly here we are staring at each other,
her gathered breath snorting like a filly,
her three fawns frozen in stillness.

In a split second they are off to the woods –
beauty floating through grass,
slender legs, white tails up,
spots on the young backs.

Soon the babies will nuzzle their mother,
sucking the good milk,
the voice of wind at their ears.

I want to watch them forever,
but what I think of most in their absence
is the brightness of the mother's eyes,
her stunned breath at the sight of me.

Among the Trees

This morning, sound changes under the oak –
a different song, a different violin.
Each leaf an arrowhead,
each notch rain and sun.

The pond through a curtain of forest,
lily's slow yellow open, lavender and golds
surround like family: cottonwood
with flying seeds, black cherry, maple,

rosebush, pussy willow.
Every crevice, stamen, and pistil
is a feast for the bee, the gold finch.
To the west, sumac shows her injury.

At her side, the ash with its silver wound
dies a slow death digesting what injures her
as if it's all right to live in the marvel of things
and die in the name of change.

Here among the trees, strong wings
and industrious feet work together.
All birth, all things that follow
take turns keeping the woods alive.

Clearing the Ditch

Today I clear the ditch's steepest slope
that covers ground with weeds, vines of grape,
shoots of elm and three-leaved poison oak,
linden limbs above that hang and drape.
A single eagle looks for a mouse to eat
in all this brush among the bits of rock.
So thick in this dreadful summer heat –
thistle, mustard, foxtail, sour dock.
I start to wonder in seldom breaks I take
if this is worth my hectic, hurried pace.
In sweat and dirt and pain, I sort and rake
this tumbled, tangled floor I bear to face.
And then I slow to hear a brown squirrel's chatter
and know all this is worth the yearly scatter.

Night Noises

Suddenly I realize that if I stepped out of my body
I would break into blossom.
— James Wright

Unnerving as the intermittent bark
    of the neighbor's English Setter,

a turkey's loud screech punctuates the air,
    settles to a soft cluck by the arbor.

High in hickories raccoons click throats
    like scolding tongues

until the timber is alive with conversation.
    Locust's lulling rhythm,

I-80's far-away purr,
    helps keep the world spinning.

My gifts in the night
    are these simple pleasures:

a breeze at my ear, a star-lit sky,
    an evening so gentle I inhale wonder.

January Rain

Experts say this is global warming –
      this burst of unusual weather,
            this surprise of Iowa rain in January.

Now that the rain has stopped,
      wind arrives like a promise tapping
            at my bedroom window. When I tuck

blankets cozy around my neck,
      the stillness of the room around me,
            I hear from its friendly tone of voice

that I can trust a breeze to do its labor,
      the task of whisking our flooded roads dry,
            finding the intricate pathways,

the graceful slide and sweep over water
      to vanish in the dark of night,
            unfolding across past and future like a ghost.

Or a lullaby in my dreams –
      this divine caretaker
            who fluffs my pillow tonight.

Watching the Herd

In the pasture, Angus,
Herefords, Holsteins graze,
each brown the shade of oak,
each black like Iowa dirt,
each white a skull-face,
until the blending begins
its mottled paisley patterns.

Heads lift to moo,
lower again to tear bluegrass.
Tails swish. Udders sag.
Cuds are chewed. Every flank
is heavy in a slow step
toward newer grass.

I want to understand, study
a believable camaraderie,
a world at peace,
but what I know
and what I see are cows,
dozens of them, moving
from east to west
at the fence line
with heifers and steers
playing at their side,
tranquil as a summer evening.

Argument for Wetlands

Old seeds cling to muskrat fur,
follow the pond turtle.
The deluge of summer floods
fills the river spill.

At dusk, a colony of egrets still their feet
among tadpoles, slip fish
down the smoothness of their necks.
I smell the wet bottom,

the new throbbing of birth,
and close in with a camera.
Mud sucking at my boots,
I frighten the waders,

watch the stunning lift of wings,
listen to the sounds
of flutter and fleeing.
Overhead, a blue heron

glides against gray sky:
neck stretched out, knees knotty,
each eye set for survival.
To my west,

gravel kicks up like exhaust fumes
behind a pickup.
Wrenches placed in a box,
brothers arrive

to fix the pump,
repair field tiling.
Their minds are on soybeans, corn.
Every thought wild to grow another crop.

Biology Field Trip; Ankeny, Iowa

Wind-borne, topsoil erodes
like gopher-eaten corn,

roots gnawed with ravenous appetite,
leaving the spoil. At this dry throat,

even the morning glory,
blue in its chokehold,

drinks the landscape's thin moisture.
Palms up like a beggar's,

Mr. Nelson explains conservation.
His hair swirls like the silt in our faces.

Tama loam wanders, steals to the river.
We resist erasure,

work to protect the soil, to silence
the cocklebur's stray, sticky bell.

Five Haiku

I.

pinprick of moonlight
a deer beside the oak tree
puppy's hard breathing

II.

wood ducks pretty perch
summer storm's quick hide-away
oak branch protection

III.

yellow crescent moon
Venus golden vase pouring
a wet dewdrop clings

IV.

sweet snowy nuthatch
frosty gray coat, winter cap
buffy warm mittens

V.

winter's bitter chill
deer feasting on willow bark
hooves growl against ice

BURN PILE

From the Edgewater Motel

for Steve

Sea light paints the underside of a gull's wing,
    a cry-like chatter over Puget Sound.

Brightness spires from a purple ridge,
    Mt. Rainier wedging into blue Seattle haze.

Across the horizon, white clouds rope
    Olympic's jagged, craggy edge.

This is your favorite vacation spot,
    the Sound's symmetrical peaks flooring

mountain summits a compatible rhythm,
    a healing respite for your chaos within.

Along Elliot Bay

Dusk slips into a black cloak
as we walk past the Victoria Clipper.
To the west of Seattle's sea,
the jagged rise of the Olympics
spires in a purple silhouette
against a salmon sunset.

On our way to the restaurant
for chicken with mojos
we are thinking of how prolific
the world is here:
the sky a thickness of gulls,
a pelican low beside the tanker,
#7 painted in red on a helicopter's side,
a Piper Cub haloing above the jellyfish –
egg yolks in the Sound.

This morning an otter amazed us,
stomach glittering above the water
like lights of holidays.
Now we're watching the cross-bars
close for the train,
hearing the draw and drag of the gears,
the ding-ding of the trolley.

A seagull drops its litter
on your Alan Stuart collar.
Like all accidents,
it comes as a surprise,
fertile, like a rumor in the air tonight
that this was inevitable,
a joke intended
for the sole purpose of laughter.

Sea Senses; Cancun, Mexico

I taste your warm salt air when I step
from veranda's bath next to you,
feel the saline touch my naked frame.

I sense your brittle chill within my bones
where I watch a fisherman on the pier
pull in a baby shark, snag a seagull's wing.

I listen to your steady roar,
know the rise and fall of your tides
like the in and out of my breathing.

I ride the small boat across your body,
fifty of us with many mother tongues,
wet from your playful splashes,
laughing and drying ourselves.

At Water's Edge

The ebb of a black shadow
exposes unexpected light

as the sun's prism
pushes into afternoon.

Our small footprints sink in sand
along the spotless beach,

each weight real
as the heavy touch hardens,

each print washing clean
in white tide fingers.

Like the seethe and retreat
of ocean waves,

our perplexities sink and rise,
regardless of the moon's enchantment.

Windstorm

This morning, the wind is sleeping.
It's a turbulent breath subsiding,
and it's good to hear
the far-off whistle of quail
from our open window.

Lifting a bean field grey as fog,
a bullied debris
across the landscape,
yesterday's gale took its toll,
every form of wildlife nestled
in their feathered, furry hatches
like anchors of common sense.

We exchange first glances.
There is work to be done –
words of acknowledgment
extended in the kitchen,
outside branches to be cleared.

We question whether wind
is errant or not,
whether our words today
will be ruinous.
Never mind, we decide,
ready to batten down
our nonchalance and passion
as a wafting breeze
rises to the occasion.

Barn Swallows

You are mowing the backyard,
the air full of swallows
diving and climbing the sky
like bombers,
catching insects on the wing.

From the deck I study their moves –
the long swoop that turns quick
for the smooth pull out sideways,
a sudden flutter of impassioned wings,
the deep scatterings.

I capture the image
of your ducking shoulder –
a swallow caught
in the repetition of a circle.

Your face churns,
even the mower's blade an agitation,
beating with its roar – a whip
that swirls and slices August grass
in the hot, dry air.

On the Ventilator

*Love is our highest word,
and the synonym of God.*
— Emerson

Steam rises from the river,
white as smoke
where cold meets warmth.

I drive on December snow
slickened by last night's thin fog,
this daily caravan to the hospital.

I want to find one doctor
reading your reports,
touching my arm at your bedside
with light in his eyes
breaking the silence of snow.

Critical Condition

Standing in the doorway
he asks to come in
and lay his hands across you.

An unlikely-looking
hospital priest –
scruffy white hair and beard,
a disheveled collar
on a young man.

Your weak nod,
and he's praying –
his hands floating
over your grave body
like silent wings.

And now
the only testament
he was here at all
is Dr. Huntwork's walking in,
saying,

Steve, your AARDS is gone.
So is your pneumonia.
We'll wean you
from the breathing tube
in the morning.

Colostomy

You hide the bright pink protrusion
like a secret under your shirt,

snapped over like Tupperware.
Even when you slumber

it sleep talks under bed sheets,
stimulates nightmares

until you think of the rupture
with each passing hour.

This is a nervous morning,
the doctor's needle sterile

in the stainless-steel drum.
You will awaken

to recovery room silence,
the words *stoma, ostomy, wafer,*

dissolving like stitches,
only threads of the haunting past.

On Being Told
You Have Cancer

Snow falling on the grasses,
the land a white-crested sea.
You tremble as you hold me

against the warmth of your skin,
the cold wrapping of the night
far from earth's hot marrow.

Your blue eyes mirroring mine,
I hear your breath's rhythm,
feel your hand on my shoulder,
heavy in trying to slow
the quickened pace of time.

After Surgery DT's

Tonight, I watch you
fold in the nurse's fingers,
try to drink her hand.
She pours a beer in your feeding tube,
checks the stable amber flow.

You hold the empty can
like a phantom love,
bring aluminum to your lips.

Tomorrow,
you will awaken hurting and tired.
Even the doctors
will feel the resistant sea wall
when they try to save you,
when they see me clinging.

How strong the suck that pulls you in,
how frightened you swim
until you are devoured
by the dark mouth
whose hunger and thirst
is never quenched.

The Commission

in memory of Steve

Leonardo da Vinci mixed pigments,
trapped glaze, varnish, oil,
until everything was cast in resin.
He was commissioned
to paint Mona Lisa's enigmatic smile,
to capture flesh like it was real,
to snare light like a shaman.
She was a silk merchant's wife
from Florence, a young mother.
It took thirty layers
to bring the world her calm.

I remember young love,
that high pedestal of perfection.
It tucked in your billfold
until the morning you died –
that favorite picture
you always carried next to your skin
like a commission of da Vinci's
that caught my most enamored smile.

Venus

I was in high school
        when you summoned me,

Venus, goddess of love,
        mother of Cupid,

who birthed full-grown
        from the foam of the Mediterranean.

He stared blue-eyed and mesmerizing
        from the hallway to my classroom,

and we were spellbound.
        After all this time it's crazy

how he slips into my dreams,
        how he is alive again, dancing,

holding me close in his arms
        like always – as you,

mistress of beauty, taught him,
        always cheek to cheek,

always the rhythm of love
        in our enchanting two-step.

Burn Pile

In today's beaming light,
this summer air, I consider
how kind the wind,
how dry the branches,
how green surrounding grass.

A bull snake slithers near my toes,
peers at me with watchful eyes.
I trust the bee at my shoulder,
pour diesel over brush,
strike the match.

This is how engines ignite,
the kindle of a spark,
a kiss of heat, and I remember
our wedding night,
the sweet burn of your love.

The fire leaps high, striking
my cheeks like a torch.
I watch the vaults
and collapses ride the air,
leave a haze in the breeze.

Soon the coals shimmer,
fade to afterglow –
the memory of what was
dusting the ground
with silver ash.

I dream you alive again,
the hearth of our touch,
your virile eyes,
and a blaze igniting
our every thought.

WOODEN SLATS
AND LAVENDER

Beginning the Day

Then it is dawn,
a crimson sun climbing the east,

doves cooing on a fence line.
She awakens to unlace her morning,

open it like a bud breaking into blossom,
but living alone is a solitary task.

When she spoons milk to her lips,
she is a bird refolding its wings.

Out the window an eagle begins its search,
ballast of air at its breast,

leaving for river fish. Light stretches
across the breakfast table, tugs her sleeve.

She presses on, dawn melting into day,
hesitant for the hunt.

The Dinner Party

I am trying to make art that relates to the deepest and
most mythic concerns of human kind and I believe that,
at this moment of history, feminism is humanism.
                                        – Judy Chicago, artist

It's hard to imagine mosquitoes
until I walk my timber today,
until I lift logs into a wagon,
tiny bites at my shoulders
and piercing the skin of my jeans.

With nothing but storms recently
mushrooms scatter the forest floor
like dinner plates
at the Brooklyn Museum.

From Sappho to O'Keeffe
the plates fill with marvel
like these gills that peek out
under caps, lopsided and soft –
the hymenophore that produces seed,
the reproductive spore.

In elm and linden vastness,
a musky scent enfolds
where yesterday's rain
has pockmarked the earth.

Not even mosquitoes can spoil
my sense of being a woman –
this place of our beautiful selves,
this sublime bed of femininity.

Mother Seed

A tender moment with my husband
and God visits my womb,
opens my fertile seed
like grain flowering –
this beginning, this gentle explosion.

The small miracle
divides his cells and grows,
a divine light arcing the dark fluid.

The faint pulse of a heartbeat
growing stronger,
the profound push out of myself
from strong thighs.

This is the turn toward selflessness,
the moment further than before –
life's dazzling birth
of other wonders to come.

Jewels in Sun

My son watches a pair of sandhill cranes
stand in last fall's cattails –
their white cheeks, red foreheads shimmering
like jewels in sun. In this swamp
they seek the smells that lure them –
minnows, tadpoles, a garter snake, a cricket.
They call in a shrill trumpet duet,
scurry up the hill to the timber.

My son films an albino deer gliding
across the neighbor's grass. He turns
to a sea of robins pulling worms from early
April thaw. Canada geese honk overhead,
honeybees leave their hives
to hover over bluebells.

My son in the goodness of it all.

The Poet

for Joe

Driving west after the rain,
I hear on the news –
The 833rd engineering unit
is being called to Iraq.

Is there a rainbow, Joe?

I ask my five-year-old grandson
when we stop along the country road.
Here, where everything
is newly bright and budding,
we get out of the car,
the rasp of gravel at our feet.
He looks up to the sky and says,

There is!

We stand together,
our breaths in whispers.
A rainbow bends to the wet earth
dazzling, sculpting the air
in a double arch
of indigos, ambers, golds.
I tell him,

The sky is a poem!

Grandma, the horse's skin jiggles
against the mosquitoes.
See her happy eyes looking at us?
Can you remember the way

she smells, her pretty back,
how the corn sings
in the windy fields?

I breathe in the magic of his words
with a hard prayer for troops
at risk of maim and dying,
etching forever this memory
of a rainbow and my grandson –
this unbreakable moment.

Tailwind

for Jacob

Wind pushes the truck bed,
a helping hand
through December streets,
when we ride to your uncle's home
for Christmas.

Moonlight spills, quivers on snow
like violin strings playing
The Blue Danube.

You are the waltz beside me,
the littlest soul
whose fingers curl the blanket,
move it away from your face.

You want to see the world
for yourself, answer each question.

You, whose innocence
teaches me the sweetness within
each musical note
with blue eyes trusting,
gaze into my care.

The Hand Stand

Trapped by a mower's blade,
my small son agonized in grass and dirt.
Father ran to the shop
for a wrench to free him.

At the hospital, his leg and foot
smelled of gasoline, blood
seeping through gauze.

After surgery,
swimming was his therapy.

Now he surfs even on lunch breaks,
his tanned skin, gray eyes
striking in Florida sun.

He's coming in on a hand stand,
that Frankenstein scar
gleaming down his leg,
his feet flashing
in a lift of the wave.

Maternity Ward

for Arlene

You are mother's milk,
your voice honey at the window
where you hold her,
birth-sweet, moonlight stroking
each golden hair.

Her blue eyes are crystal,
eyelashes long as the future,
the crooked little toes –
each masterpiece the witness
of something pure,
something phenomenal.

Radiance circles
the small round of her head.
Her breath dances on your ear.
Your arms wrap around her
tight as love.

Resilience

for Ryla

Paradise Beach
is where the shark attacked –
ocean's roar at her ears,
cascades of tide rushing to shore.

Perhaps her board hit the beast.
Perhaps it reacted
like a dog defending its bone.

Whatever it was,
her foot has mended now.
She surfs the Florida tide –
a mermaid reaching sand,
climbing back out again.

She trusts the glide across water,
lifts above fear
as if balancing life is enough,
as if risk is simply worth the ride.

Epithalamium

for Barbara and Sharpe

Today, this day was a brimming cup,
today, this day was the immense wave,
today, it was all the earth.
— Pablo Neruda

By the tall larkspur,
balsam, azalea's flame,
swallows quiet overhead,
turn in the sky.

A distant voice of thunder
echoes through aspen,
spruce saplings, Douglas fir,

shaping your vows
into the forever song,
I Will Always Love You.

Wooden Slats and Lavender

in memory of Gary

When my brother visited
our home in the woods tonight
to borrow our Chevy truck,
he said his wife's mother
was giving them the porch swing
she didn't need –
wooden slats
that rocked on a base.

My brother wanted it on the deck,
but his wife whispered a kiss
into the back of his neck,
told him she wanted it
under the willow by the garden,
near the red raspberries,
thyme, lavender, and petunias.

Doesn't he know
wooden slats and rhythm
mark the sway of a heartbeat?
And that if he brushed
across her softness
as they sat outlined
in Grandfather's pine
near the Jonathan apple trees,
scatterings of climbing tomato vines,
cauliflower wrapped and tied
to avoid the stain of the sun,
and silver sparks
falling on their bare feet,
the very meaning of life itself
would be in his hands?

The Drive

Snow moon's melt into South Dakota sky,
my brother drives to the hospital.
He steps from the car, scuffs his boots
on concrete with the weight of a train.

Sometimes we don't think about death
until things start declining,
like this siege attacking my brother's heart
until the doctor, in surgery,
watches it almost shut down.

Now he can't see out his window
overlooking the parking lot, can't see
the turkey's long, red caruncles
where the tom struts through crisp
January air. Too many tubes
are tying him down, filling and draining.

Today in the center of everything
is a secret only God perceives –
mile after mile, knowing my brother
is ready for whatever comes,
my brother is ready for the drive ahead.

Bypass

Before the surgeon sees my brother's
damaged heart, before the ventilator
bides its long, lonely hours, my brother
asks the nurse if she has any sage.

This is South Dakota where he says
the children at the reservation are starving.
Starving. And he wants the blessing
that fills the pouch with prayer

to chant his heart to heal,
to beat like the reservation drums
where children dream food, dream warmth
from the unforgiving winter.

Tonight at the hospital, my brother dreams
the rhythm of the eagle's wing
as it stirs the flowered sky. My brother
questions, *Is it time? Is it time?*

Midnight Train

in memory of Mother

The midnight train rolls through
this sleepy town like a clock

you could set your watch by.
I love the warning drawl of the whistle,

the rattle and roll of iron on iron,
but at this time of night

it's more of a lull to someone's dream
than fierceness, more company

than anything to those of us who can't sleep.
My mother is a precious flower

in the next bedroom. Even awake
she can't hear the constant rumble

along the tracks, can't remember
destinations or commerce,

can't distinguish if it's the month of June.
But she remembers me,

the one who stays in her hour of need.
And what more is there,

after all, in life's scheme
than the simple beauty of aging as it unfolds.

Under My Care

in memory of my father-in-law,
Bob Underwood

Even the sheet's fray is turned
with the smooth side touching your skin.

I have carefully tucked pillows
under your elbow's bend

and beneath the backs of your heels.
Coleus and Norfolk pine

line the family room,
our pictures facing your bed.

I adjust your elevation,
check the draw sheet's position,

the rhythm of your breathing.
You whisper,

When is the end of the world?
Your green eyes pin me tight

for an answer. *I don't know,* I say
and stumble to the sofa.

With the lamp on,
I see your face lit in a halo.

At midnight you call my name,
and like a hummingbird drinking

a rose's last sweetness,
I hover over your bones.

Sabbatical Homes, London

for George

White window frame,
soft flutter of ivy outside,

where summer air sifts quiet
through the room.

Hospitality tucks
within each towel's fold

for us to wrap in after bathing,
the water magical against our skin.

This is how someone
lends a home, how we soak

in the luxury of each other.
The time we have together –

the time beyond beautiful.

Lady Liberty

The Hudson at our ears,
our tour boat glides close.
New York Harbor opens its mouth,
and we click our cameras,
sway with the current.

She's a lighthouse warning ships
from rocky shoals,
a beacon lighting the narrows,
a statue with a staircase inside.

She wears crown jewels,
rests her feet on old Fort Wood
with its sally port and thick walls,
this woman with her golden lamp,
eloquent against March sky.

How many cloaks she wears –
like a mother who gathers us
into her fold. *Give me your tired,
your poor*, she says until grace
shivers through our bones.

We swing back to see her again,
necks bent, eyes glistening
at the entrance that forever welcomes,
the arm that forever lifts,
the torch that forever burns.

In this Ethiopian restaurant

we're a mosaic,
the batik on the wall
where all colors drape as one.

We tear soft African bread,
gather chicken, cabbage,
green beans, mushrooms
with our fingers.

It's been fifty years since
King's *I have a dream!*

We sip our tea,
the fragrance from the platter
succulent. Our stomachs fill
and families line up
to take our seats.

Here, there's enough equality
to sustain a future, enough
pots in the kitchen
steaming to overcome.

A Night in Brooklyn

In Park Slope we order
sea bass with parsley sauce.
Served on leaves,
the bass swims in shallots and butter.
We raise sauvignon blanc –
elegant with sun-ripened grapes
hand-picked from the vine,
aged like an old woman with fine skin.

We walk into the clear night air,
smell bagels and coconut shrimp,
touch the market's cantaloupes,
watch nighthawks roughhouse
around a light pole. Near traffic
a man stumbles into another man,
eyes silvery under black hats,
a cry of Yiddish.

At Rite Aid a barefoot shopper
mumbles to cough drops
that she's been accosted then whispers
something to the Band-Aids.
Wearing a pastel burqa
the clerk asks a woman in line
if we can use that lady's card
for a discount.

We slip into a taxi and hear
America's voice in an Indian accent.
Where to? he asks.
We soak up this world that is ours,
liberty herself welcoming all
who live, die, and pass through here –
a few we meet along the way.

Trinity

This is for those who feel
something beyond –

a thing inexplicable,
like a word

always the shadow
of an unspoken word,

the nursing hand
enfolding the fevered hand,

the ashes of good works
never moral enough.

So incredible
is this power,

so bright this promise.
The dove,

radiant in flight,
splashes against the sun.

About the Author

Pat Underwood grew up on an Iowa farm, married her high school sweetheart, and together they raised two sons on a country hillside northwest of Colfax, Iowa where the plentiful wildlife inspired many of her poems. After receiving her college degree at the age of 44, she worked in early education and retired in 2017 from her employment with the State of Iowa. Former publications include two poetry chapbooks – *Portraits* (Finishing Line Press 2017) and *Gatherings* (Celestial Light Press 2007). Her play kit *The Last Supper* (Meriwether Publishing Ltd.; Contemporary Drama Service 1997) travels the nation. Underwood's poems received a 2001 Pushcart Prize Nomination, a 1996 Founder's Award, and a 2002 Founder's Award from the National Federation of State Poetry Societies.

www.ingramcontent.com/pod-product-compliance
Lightning Source LLC
Chambersburg PA
CBHW031929080426
42734CB00007B/616